Wicca

Candle Magic

*An Introductory Modern Guide to
Wiccan Spells, Rituals, Witchcraft and
Magic for the Solitary Practitioner using
Candles and Fire*

Lisa Woods

Table of Contents

INTRODUCTION

Starting Out Your Journey to Tarot Reading

We all start our journey to tarot in different ways; different circumstances lead different people to tarot reading. Inevitably, people are going to view the very practice of tarot reading from different individual perspectives. The most difficult fact to accept about tarot reading, however, is the fact there is no absolute right or wrong way to carry out specific actions, or to make certain deductions from tarot cards.

Unlike other more accurate scientific fields, tarot reading is an art that has thrived over the ages on generating controversies in interpretations; bringing people together using differences in their reasoning. So, the way you are going to understand how the reading of a particular card or spread appears to your peculiar situation might differ slightly from how even your reader would see it.

They key to being a great tarot reader in the long run, therefore, is for you first to find yourself, and come to terms with who you are. You need to realize exactly who you are, underneath the cloak of educational backgrounds, social class and all those cloaks we use to mask our real selves in the modern society. You are not your occupation or job description, you are not your position in your family, you are not the role that the society has foisted on you.

You must go back to the very basics of your consciousness and discover who you are and the ideals you hold dear. Discovering yourself will help you to have an independent voice and a self-reliant thought pattern that will be able to help your intuition bloom. Once you as a person are in perfect harmony with your intuition, then reading the cards and relating them to your personal life becomes easier.

Discovering yourself will also let you find out you are intrinsically different from everybody else. Who you are fundamentally as a person differs from what people think you are, and it sure differs from who other people are? Therefore, since we all different on a very primal, basal level, it is not expected for our intuitions to work the same way. What your intuition regards the interpretation of a card to mean in your situation is likely to be slightly different from what someone else would think if they got that particular reading in your same situation. So, self-discovery will let you understand who you are, and will let you come to terms with the differences that exist between yourself and others.

Now that you have understood that the basic requirement is knowing who you are to enable your intuition to bloom unrestricted, the next step is for you to learn the basics of Tarot. For a tarot reading to be carried out, five basic pre-requisites must be in place. First and most importantly. There should be a reader. If there is no reader, then exactly how is the interpretation of the card going to be determined? So, a reader has to be in place to examine the cards drawn and the spread created, and to guide the person who asks the question on the core meaning of the reading produced.

This leads to our second most important factor, the querent. In Tarot literature, a querent is simply the person who asks the question (or who makes the query). In circumstances of personal divination therefore, the reader and the querent are going to be the same person. So, the querent is the one who is seeking an answer to a burning problem.

The third pre-requisite is the question itself. This is the most important thing the querent has to possess for a tarot reading to be successful – a concise, clear-cut question that has been decided on in advance or on the spot. For a querent to be able to relate a tarot reading to his circumstances, the question asked has to be as concise and unambiguous as possible.

The next most important pre-requisite is the deck of cards. There are different types of tarot cards in existence currently, but the most common and most widely accepted tarot deck is the Rider-Waite-Smith tarot deck. The original version of this deck was first created in 1909, and its simplicity and conciseness has endeared it to the hearts of many tarot readers over the years. This has made it the deck of choice for both avid tarot enthusiasts and beginners who are just starting in the game of tarot reading.

The whole tarot deck can be divided into two major sections, the major arcana, or the major mysteries, and the minor arcana, or the minor mysteries. The cards in both sections of the deck will be explained in detail as we move on.

Finally, a spread is the last important pre-requisite for a reading to be completed. A spread may be an arrangement of cards picked out in a particular fashion based on the direction of the reader's or querent's intuition. In other types of readings, the spread may be a single card pulled randomly from a deck or a random pile of cards. Whatever form it takes, the most important thing to note is that the spread is the card, or sequence of cards that is interpreted to answer the question asked by the querent.

Even though a lot of tarot readers practice personal divination in the modern dispensation, back in ancient Europe, there were huge concerns about the ability of readers to be objective when seeking answers to their questions from the cards. So, when carrying out a personal divination through a tarot reading, as both the reader and the querent, you need to strive consciously during the tarot reading to remain as objective as possible when carrying out the reading.

Of course, as stated earlier, there is no specific way to interpret a spread. People examine core meanings, and then relate them to their specific situations based on their convictions. So, whether you like it or not, your convictions about that question you asked will come into play as you seek answers from the cards. It is now up to you as a reader to look deeply at the core meanings of the cards in your spread, and make an objective deduction based on your intuition, and not a deduction that aligns with your wishes.

Since the heyday of Tarot reading, the practice has never been seen as a form of inquiry from an absolute supernatural source. Tarot reading have always been regarded as a way of providing a mirror for us to gaze back unto ourselves, our unique predicaments, circumstances and situations and reflect deeply to come up with intuitive deductions and solutions. Tarot aims to help you reach into the deepest recesses of your mind, and relate the tarot reading you have done by yourself, or the one an expert reader has just done for you to your unique circumstances.

It's that simple. Having to distill the path to the solution of your problems to just one image or a few sequential images allows you to think deeply from a unique perspective. See how the core meanings of the card relate to you, and begin to work out a simple, basic solution to your problems. Tarot helps to eliminate complexities by forcing you to come down to a basal level when attempting to solve a problem. Instead of engaging your analytical mind and trying to find various complex solutions to mostly simple problems, tarot brings your intuitive mind into the picture. It allows you build your solutions from the simple to the complex phases, which is the most efficient mechanism of problem solving.

Contrary to popular opinion, you don't need to have studied the entire tarot deck to be able to perform a simple reading. The key to a successful tarot reading is your intuition; the limitless power of your mind. So, as a total novice with no prior knowledge of tarot, you can still carry out an effective tarot reading using the power of your intuition. All you have to do is get your deck of cards (you can do that right now if you have your deck with you), think of a particular question, pull out a single card (we don't want any complications yet), and then think of how the image on the card relates to the question you asked.

You can just write down the first couple of things that comes to your mind. It might take a while for you to be able to effectively establish a connection between the question you asked and the image on the card you pulled. That's where the power of your intuitive mind comes in. The more you ponder intuitively on the image, the clearer the path between your tarot reading and the question you asked becomes to you. It's so simple, yet so unbelievably powerful.

Finally, we'll be looking at how to read a spread appropriately. The spread, is the layout of the cards that allows the reader to provide an answer to the querent's question using his interpretation of the core meanings of the cards and the sequence in which the cards appear. Sometimes, the sequence of the cards may not be put into consideration, it all eventually boils down to your intuition.

Most tarot readers like to use a three-card spread. The first card represents the events of the past, the second represents the events of the present, while the third represents how the past and present will lead to a particular future occurrence. For some readings, only once card is used, and in some readings, more than three cards are used. No hard and fast rules apply.

Chapter 1:
Meaning of The Cards and Cards Interpretation Part 3

The Hanged Man

THE HANGED MAN.

"I can't fight or force the things that I cannot control. For this reason, I surrender."

Love

The Hanged Man indicates that you are in a state of limbo; there is no movement forward or backward—you're just hanging around, waiting in suspension and suspense. You may need to abandon any expectations for the relationship temporarily at this time—pause and not force or rush anything. If you are ready to move forward with a relationship, The Hanged Man could indicate that your partner may not have the same idea or that you are fearful of speaking the truth from your heart. For singles, it may seem like there is no progress in your dating life—or at least not the kind you may have been hoping for. This card reminds you to trust that the universe is holding you in good hands and doesn't want you to move forward for a reason. Let go of your need to control.

Career/Work

The Hanged Man symbolizes feelings of powerlessness regarding your work situation. You may find yourself waiting for a message or for something to materialize. This card can also suggest letting go of your need to control, instead being more open to taking direction from others and hearing different points of view.

Personal/Spiritual

The Hanged Man in personal readings is incredibly powerful because it shows that learning to let go and trust in something bigger than yourself will lead to your highest and greatest good. This card reminds you to have faith in yourself and the universe. Believe it or not, it is possible to enjoy this limbo phase if you relax into it and know that this will make the progress that much faster!

Reversed

When reversed, The Hanged Man shows that you are struggling to maintain control, refusing to let go to the point where it has become a detriment to your well-being. You may be fighting the inevitable or refusing to see things for what they are out of fear or a resistance to moving forward into the future. On the other hand, this card can signify that you may be staying in a space of helplessness and making yourself a victim.

Death

DEATH.

"I'm experiencing a period of incredible transformation!"

Death is the card of total and complete transformation. It is one of my favorites within the Major Arcana because when this card appears, it reveals that the circumstances around you have entered into a cycle of purging, cleansing, and releasing. Something around you now is coming to completion to make room for new growth. Wherever there is an ending, there is always a beginning, and the Death card is a symbolic representation of that process occurring in your life now. With any kind of "death," that energy is born anew in some other form. You may be releasing toxic people, thoughts, or things; moving from one place to the next; or saying goodbye to someone or something for now.

Love

The Death card symbolizes the end of some aspect of the relationship. Your love life is totally changing and revamping itself. It's possible that this can bring feelings of sadness, but at the same time, I have seen this card (very often!) show up for people who were moving from one phase of love to another or saying goodbye to singledom and welcoming love into their lives.

Career/Work

Your career and work life are under a spell of transformation when the Death card shows up. Something is coming to an end and the universe is preparing you for a new beginning. This card is a wonderful sign if you have been setting intentions to create a major change in your life, but if you are to be laid off from your job, it can definitely bring disappointment, too. Either way, you are reaching an end, experiencing a cut of some sort and being asked to be flexible as this transformation takes place.

Personal/Spiritual

You are laying to rest aspects of your life that no longer serve you, as indicated by the Death card. You may be forced out of a situation or find yourself in the midst of a total transformation as parts of your life melt away and take on a new form. With Death, it's important to remain open to these changes, even if they seem to your detriment initially.

Reversed

When reversed, the Death card can signify that you are avoiding necessary change. You may be holding on to something or grieving to the point where you have stopped experiencing the magick of your own life. Remember, every ending is the beginning of a new journey that will bring gifts all of its own. Resisting change doesn't stop it from happening, but it can and will prolong suffering.

Temperance

TEMPERANCE.

"I am working to bring opposite energies together to create something new."

Temperance signifies that this is a major moment to bring balance, moderation, and alchemy into your life. This card represents taking two very separate and different things and bringing them together to create some new form. This requires trial and error, which is why this card also symbolizes patience. Balance is needed, but in the eyes of the Temperance card, balance doesn't have to be a 50/50 split. It means finding the right mix of elements that works for you or helps you meet your goal. These two elements can be two people from different backgrounds or with different lifestyles. Either way, the appearance of the Temperance card means they are now working to come together in a magical new form in a way that's best for them.

Love

Temperance is about two people trying to figure out how to merge together. It represents patience but also respect for each other's differences, including finding out what works best for you both. You may be experimenting with different ways of communicating or working your schedules to make time for each other. If you are single, it may signify that you need to be patient with the universe as it works to find your "better half" for you. Take your time, the Temperance card says—don't try to rush to work things out. Patience is needed now more than ever, as well as understanding and an open mind.

Career/Work

When Temperance appears, you are trying to find balance or a system that works for you at your workplace. You may be trying out ideas, trying on new roles, or working with totally different groups of people to bring a project or goal to completion. Because there are so many different variables involved, you want to make room for some trial and error and not expect perfection right out of the gate. If you learn more about the project or the people involved with it, you will find you have a better shot at moving forward and creating something special and unique. Remember, patience is always needed with the Temperance card, no matter the question asked.

Personal/Spiritual

The Temperance card signals a need for moderation and balance. Where in your life does there seem to be too much or too little? Now is the time to rework this chemistry in a way that makes you feel better and supports your ability to thrive, not just survive. This card gives you permission to slow down, forgive yourself and others, and take it easy. You can also find yourself working out a balance within yourself—between your shadow side and light side—or trying to find where you fit in the world and who or what belongs beside you.

Reversed

When reversed, the Temperance card is symbolic of some kind of extreme. Balance is lost—there is either too much or not enough of something. We see this card when we are overindulging, worn down and not resting, or forcing an issue. Also, sometimes two different things are not destined to come together or to work, at least not now. Reversed, this card suggests that the differences are just too great to blend successfully. Find something else or pause to restore order once more.

Chapter 2:
Meaning of The Cards and Cards Interpretation Part 4

The Devil

Astrological Association: Capricorn

Kabbalah Path: Ayin, the Eye

The Devil shows a carelessness of results. In a way, he shows the ecstasy in all material things, but also how far they can drag us down.

There is a simple joy in indulging the desires, of cutting loose and letting wild. On its surface, there is nothing wrong with that. The problem with the Devil is that he is indiscriminate in what he indulges in. He revels in it all, be it healthy or poison, and does not suffer from a moral dilemma. He does not care what is right or wrong, only what makes him feel good. The Devil tempts with his simple joy, and when you're not looking, binds you to worldly pleasures he offers. He shows the short-sighted view of pursuing what you want without regarding the consequences. He also shows the abandonment of the spiritual. One does not need to be an ascetic to fulfill their spirit, but the Devil's trap is an easy one to fall into, and if not careful, the worldly can replace the spiritual very quickly.

The Devil comes and offers you a drink. "It's a long Journey, you should take a break and have fun for a while," he says. You join him, and one drink turns into another, then another, then another, for many days. It feels so good and easy at the time. But one night you pass out, and when you wake up, you find a chained shackle around your ankle. The Devil stands over you, chain in hand. "You've done so much already. Do you really need to keep struggling? You should just stay here," he says, offers you another drink.

Meanings

Instant gratification is the Devil's mantra. This is you giving over to your shadow side and allowing bad decisions to rule your life. You are stuck in the rut of the patterns of your behavior. At his worst, he often shows addiction or abuse, even violence. His appearance in a reading shows the chains that bind you from living as your best self. However, in seeing the chains, you are that much closer to freeing yourself of them.

Shadow Aspect

The Devil has fully blinded you. Under his influence, you have grown weak and allowed your petty desires to own you fully. As a result, you suffer the consequences.

The Tower

Astrological Association: Mars

Kabbalah Path: Peh, the Mouth

More than the Death card, this is the sign that makes a tarot reader sweat. The Tower is a swift catastrophe. In this card, everything is annihilated.

The Tower is that which shakes your fundamental understanding of the universe. All the rules you have lived by thus far are shown to be lies and you are left without a leg to stand on. More than at any other time, you are left disoriented. How can you be sure of what to rely on when everything can come crashing down at a moment's notice? As painful as if may be, this is the quintessential core of spiritual awakening. It is similar to concepts from Eastern philosophy, in which Nothingness is perfection, and so all manifestations of this world, for good or evil, are blights upon Nothingness. The Tower, then, becomes the vehicle of emancipation from the existence that traps us. Its destruction shows you how foolish it was to cling to it in the first place. Life is all an illusion. Not even your ego means anything. The Tower strips you of everything so that you may see nothing within everything.

The Devil has you imprisoned in a Tower. He binds you there by placating you with an easy life and tells you how wise you are. So, you stay. Every once in a while, you think about your

Journey and see the path of it from your window, but always you turn back to the comfort of the Tower. The Journey was difficult, and you learned enough. Life here is good. Then, lightning strikes. In a rain of fire, it comes crumbling down, and the only way to save yourself is to leap from the window. You land on your Journey's path and watch as everything in which you found solace is destroyed. At that moment, you realize that all that matters is being present in the moment.

Meanings

This card heralds' imminent calamity. Utter ruin is foreseen, and the misery of having to pick up the pieces. The confusion will destabilize everything you've ever known.

Shadow Aspect

This card is one in which the shadow aspect actually brings out the good in it. In this case, this means spiritual enlightenment. You've seen the chaos around you and used it as a means of personal growth. You now see the facade and become aware of the true value in things.

The Star

Astrological Association: Aquarius

Kabbalah Path: Tzaddi, the Fish Hook

After the apocalypse of the Tower, in the light of the Star, we see the Truth revealed in its full light. She is the gifts of the Spirit flowing freely.

The Star brings immortality in that there is no separation between the core of the Self and the Divine Spirit. She embodies the personal growth that happens after the Tower. This is the soul who withstood the worst and came out its best. This is because, with the Star, all things are fully understood and appreciated for what they are, be they good or evil. Everything has a purpose in this world. In her light, blessings flow forth, and the farthest Star is within reach.

Through the razing of the Tower, your Journey has stripped of all that kept you from what you are at the center of your being. The ego has been dissolved and you exist in your purest sense. The Star shines down on you and pours the Divine down onto you like water. Faith is your power.

Meanings

Its most basic interpretation is hope in the sense that the Star shows bright prospects. That's only a surface reading, though. The Star represents much more. The Divine is everywhere, and you are connected to it. One does not need hope when united fully and totally to Spirit. Remain open to the gifts pouring down on you.

Shadow Aspect

There's an arrogance here, an attitude of being higher-than-thou. This is not true spiritual inspiration. If your faith is tested, you may find it to be shaken easily until the Star can shine through for real.

The Moon

Astrological Association: Pisces

Kabbalah Path: Koph, the Mind

This is the dark night of the soul. After the enlightenment found in the Star, after that blissful, perfect fulfillment, the soul swings back into doubt and fear. This is the power of the Moon.

This is a time when it will feel like you're feeling your way through the dark. The Moon is the unknown. This kind of pressure raises the animal instinct in all of us and so the natural response of fear. This is all subconscious activity of the deep processes that drive us. In defense of the intensity of the previous two cards, the subconscious draws up veils again and makes us see bogeymen where there are only shadows. Now, more than ever, our intuition is our only guide.

The brightness of the Star fades, and you are only left with the light of the Moon on your Journey. You stumble and fall, and freeze in fear. Everywhere around you, danger lurks and wolves howl. You don't know how you will ever make it through. But deep within you, something pushes you along, makes you look twice at the shadows. You begin to see they are just branches moving in the wind, and that the wolves are just dogs alert to your presence. Uneasily, you move through your fear and push forward through the night.

Meanings

This card serves to show you that there may be many things hidden deep within your psyche that are rearing their head. You may not know what they are exactly, but they are affecting you, and you feel their presence. This card embodies uncertainty and fear. Things are never what they seem under the light of the Moon.

Shadow Aspect

This is the silence when you know there should be sound. There is still an element of fear, but this silence only brings out what is unknown. You know there are intuitive messages coming your way, but you can't hear them. And yet, you're still afraid, because you know there's something out there you need to be aware of. Be still and listen harder.

Chapter 3:
Meaning of The Cards and Cards Interpretation Part 5

The Sun

Astrological Association: The Sun

Kabbalah Path: Resh, the Head

The Sun exposes all visions for what they are and detangles all mysteries. It is the most positive card in the deck and shines its light on everything around it.

Rather than the subconscious rising up, this is complete consciousness. This is the soul in full realization of itself. There is a certain simplicity in this card, of just being what it is, the warmth and joy and energy of all happiness made manifest. The subconscious and the conscious are joined as one. The soul goes forth as a whole being.

After the night comes the dawn. The Sun rises over the horizon, chasing away all shadows and leaving the Journey clear for you ahead. You bask in its light, allow the warmth to charge you, and with a deep breath, continue on your path in its light.

Meanings

This is a time when you can share the absolute best of yourself. This card has a lot of energy in it and may indicate a period where you will be so full to brim you won't know what to do with yourself. Life is good with this card. If you're looking for a 'yes' in your reading, this is a 'yes' shouted from the mountaintops.

Shadow Aspect

Everything is exposed in the light of the Sun. Some things may come to light that may not be pleasant to look at. However, the Sun is a uniformly positive card, even in negative contexts, so this exposure is always a good thing, like hanging something out in the sun to air out. Nothing can ruin this beautiful day.

Judgment

The judgment card is a call to stop and stare long and hard at your life and how it has been going. When it comes up in a reading, this card reminds us that we are working towards a future and what the future is can change at any moment. If you want to work in movies but ended up in TV because you thought it was your way in, it is more than okay to change your goal to something related to this new circumstance. You can aim for whatever kind of future you want; it is entirely up to you at any moment. You are the emperor of your own life; you get to decide. Because of this, you also know that you can change and leave your past self behind. That doesn't need to continue existing and holding you down. These are powerful reminders that will help greatly. When you see the judgment card, you should take some time to reflect on where you have come from and where you are now. Then consider where you want to be. How far have you come, and what do you need to do to get there? Is it still something you want, or is it time to set a new future? All of these are under your control, and the judgment card reminds us to recalibrate these values so we can get a better understanding of who we are and live more fully in line with our values.

The World

The world represents everything, and this means the end of the fool's journey; every desire has been achieved. Each part of the tarot deck so far has either been about a part of you or the way that events are going to play out. The world represents you as each of these parts combined into a single whole. You are every other card and the lessons they hold, now in a single card. When the world is drawn, you know that you are doing well and that the road you are walking is leading you directly to your unique destiny as a complete individual. However, as wonderful as this is, it needs to be remembered that this is referring to the question being asked of the tarot cards and not just life as a whole. So, the world points towards the answer, the positive outcome, the resolution of an issue. Whether it ends poorly or well, it ended the way it needed to end for you to continue on the path you are on. The world is a treasured card because it comes at the end of the deck. The deck doesn't end on a downer. Life is an extraordinary thing according to the fool's journey, and there are hard lessons to be learned, but they're what gives us greater power over our lives, and this is a truly excellent way to end the major arcana.

Chapter 4:
Meaning of The Cards and Cards Interpretation Part 6

Suit of Cups

The suit of cups deals with emotional energy. When these cards appear, it's time to examine your relationships, feelings, and whether your amount of emotional expression is appropriate. When trying to make a decision, cups tell you to let your heart and your "gut" guide you.

Ace of Cups

Ylang-Ylang EO

When this card appears in a reading, you are channeling loving energy from a higher power. Look around, because the Universe is trying to give you a gift. Receive this loving energy and let that love flow through you into the world around you. The energy of all Aces is the energy of new beginnings. The Ace of Cups can indicate a new relationship, a new creative opportunity, or a call to show your compassionate side. Know that if you say "yes" to these new endeavors you will experience great emotional fulfillment. This card is a call to open your heart and allow love to flow to you and through you.

Two of Cups

This card is a symbol of partnership, but because all cups cards deal with emotions, this is a very loving union. Whether a romantic partner, a business partner or a best friend, you are on the same energetic frequency with another person. Right now, you're in the early stages of your relationship, but this is likely going to be a long-term connection. Your similarities are in deep alignment and your differences complement each other well. Keep your eyes open for this potential new relationship and if you have found it - nurture it.

Three of Cups

Loyalty EO blend

When the Three of Cups appears in a tarot reading, it's a sign that you need to connect with your tribe. So much can be gained from time spent with good friends: from filling each other up with love and support to providing inspiration or collaborating on a project. It is often around your closest friends that you can let go of inhibitions and temporarily step away from your day-to-day stresses. This is not a time to take turns complaining, but instead it's a time to truly lift each other up and celebrate with joy and optimism. If it's hard to identify the group of people who make you feel this way, this card may be a sign to seek out a group of like-minded people or start a group of your own.

Four of Cups

Grounding EO blend

When the Four of Cups appears in a reading, it's a sign that you may need to say "No" to certain invitations and opportunities. By declining an offer now, you'll be in a better place to say "Yes" to new experiences later. You may be eager to take any opportunity that comes along because you're feeling bored and unfulfilled, but this card is telling you to wait for a better option. You may just have too much on your plate right now and you need to say "No" to avoid overwhelm. Give yourself permission to sit this one out. This is the time to examine your deeper purpose and passions so that you can focus your energy in the right direction. One caution - make sure you're not saying "No" out of fear or because your expectations are unrealistic. While you don't want to accept something that you know isn't a good fit, you also don't want to turn away every opportunity because you can find a minor flaw.

Five of Cups

Acceptance EO blend

The Five of Cups is a sign of disappointment. A situation didn't turn out as you expected and now you can't stop thinking about how you could have changed the outcome. You may also be focused on the unfairness of the situation and where others let you down or did you wrong. It's ok to feel disappointed, but when this card appears, it's a sign to start wrapping up the pity party and moving forward. Forgive yourself and others. Learn from mistakes that were made and if others showed their true colors, learn from that too. Often when things go wrong it's easy to focus on just the negative, but were there some positives too? Look for

the people who stepped up during this situation and the new opportunities that became available because of the change of direction.

Six of Cups

Inner Child EO blend

When this card appears in a reading, it often symbolizes a connection with people and places from your past. It's a call to reconnect with the energy of happier and less complicated times. Consider brightening someone's day with a random act of kindness. If there was an activity you loved to do years ago - painting, dancing, singing - try it again now. Make yourself and others smile today. This is a fantastic time to be playful and creative with no concern about how you'll be judged by others. Approach projects and relationships without expectation or prejudice. If your childhood was an unpleasant time, use this as an opportunity to nurture your inner child. Use affirmations to speak love to the younger version of yourself who lives within you. Say the words you longed to hear and give yourself the love you never received.

Seven of Cups

When the Seven of Cups appears in a Tarot reading, it's a sign that you are facing multiple choices or opportunities. When you're presented with too many options, it can actually be more confusing than beneficial. Take a close look at each of the choices in front of you. If something seems too good to be true, it probably is. Beware of abandoning your current project in favor of something else just because it's new and shiny. Instead of focusing on the promised outcome, make a plan for how you will achieve this success and decide whether that plan is something you can really commit to. This card is also a reminder that sooner rather than later you DO need to make a choice. Time will be wasted if you wait for the answer to become clear instead of actively exploring your options.

Citronella EO can be beneficial in improving focus when you're feeling "wishy washy." Apply to the corresponding alarm point:

at the junction between the base of the skull and the top of the spine at the back of the neck.

Eight of Cups

When the Eight of Cups appears in a tarot reading you are walking away from something that no longer serves you. This will be difficult because it means letting go of something you once loved. Unfortunately, you've realized that this situation, opportunity, or relationship isn't truly in line with your desires and ultimate goals, and it likely never will be. You are not experiencing the spiritual or emotional fulfillment' you were hoping to achieve, so it's no longer worth staying. Use this to card as a sign to seek out what brings true happiness into your life, even if that means a tough goodbye. The only caution is to be sure that you aren't running away simply to avoid addressing a difficult situation. If it doesn't serve you, move on. If you leave solely to dodge an uncomfortable issue, you will likely encounter that same predicament repeatedly until you finally deal with it.

Nine of Cups

The Nine of Cups calls you to express gratitude for all the blessings in your life. When this card appears, the results you've been working and praying for in your work, relationships, and within yourself are coming to fruition. Enjoy this time and appreciate all that you have. Remember that you will attract more blessings when your grateful energy is sensed by the universe. Consider seeking out ways to share your abundance with others, as your generosity will be similarly rewarded. If you're experiencing financial success, reward yourself with a purchase that makes you happy. If you've found love, let yourself be swept away for the weekend. Good times will come and go. Fully experiencing this time of abundance will refresh your soul and make the difficult times easier.

Ten of Cups

It symbolizes genuine happiness within your family and relationships. You share love, joy and deep connections. When this card appears in a reading, look for opportunities to spend more time, emotions, and experiences with your loved ones.

Page of Cups

The Page of Cups signals a spark of inspiration the messages might not make sense at first but as you remain open to new information the pieces will begin to come together.

Knight of Cups

Upright - A youth who is flirty, romantic, sensitive, kind, loving, poetic, idealistic, an invitation, the hero or knight in shining armor, possibly fickle, love offering or engagement.

Reversed - Love interest moving away, sight is on another or another thing, emotional distraction, chasing dreams or fantasies, idealism, hopeless romantic who can never find perfection and therefore is not reliable or committed.

Queen of Cups

Upright - A woman who is sensitive, kind, loving, romantic, idealistic, maternal, intuitive, psychic, deep, spiritual, nurturing, emotional, could be a psychic reader.

Reversed - Self-effacing, too shy, gifted but too timid or weak to trust in yourself, needs not being met, needs emotional support and nourishment, very psychic but not speaking it, no one is listening.

King of Cups

Upright - A man who is kind, sensitive, loving, romantic, likes water, intuitive, psychic, nurturing, emotional, sometimes unstable, generally good natured, needs to be able to relax and integrate his experiences and feelings.

Reversed - Needs some time out for self-reflection, retreat near water, be careful near water, solo is best for a while, wise counselor, deep feeling and kind, genuinely concerned for the welfare of

others, may seem aloof.

CUPS people usually have blonde hair and blue or green or green eyes.

Their astrological signs most often are Pisces, Cancer and Scorpio.

Chapter 5:
Meaning of The Cards and Cards Interpretation The Swords

Ace of Swords

Upright - Onrush of swift and powerful energy, bringing clarity or courage or causing someone to act in a quick and decisive way for good or ill, cutting through, force, double-edged sword, use force wisely.

Reversed - Death to a person or situation, 'no' is the answer, inability to decide, conflict is ruining clarity of choice, put down the sword and call a truce, don't use force or aggression unwisely,

peace is a two-edged sword, be graceful and gentle, but firm, time to give

something or someone a rest.

2 of Swords

Upright - Caught between two choices, perceptions or opinions, unable to decide, temporary truce, stalemate, neutrality, having blinders on, poise, unsure of the outcome, other forces at work in the situation, pointing the finger at someone, not wanting to be involved.

Reversed - Staying balanced and firm in a difficult situation, holding 2 points of view of equal value, waiting for something to blow over, time will tell what will be decided, waiting patiently for the outcome.

3 of Swords

Upright - Heartbreak involving two or more people, love triangle, sorrow, loss, separation, breakup, abortion or miscarriage, grief, sometimes in the past rather than the present or future, the ending of a relationship, past, present or future, suffering from others affecting you, need to withdraw from a situation or from circumstance which does not involve you, need for self-recovery.

Reversed - Let the past go, healing from emotional trauma or wounds, good health, having much love to give, heart operations successful, forgive others, bad weather for travel, beware of accident potentials, don't let other's drive your car.

Upright - Retreat, rest from strife, recuperation,

hospitalization, meditation, solace, needed healing, peace and tranquility, things on hold, timing not right for action, reviewing religious beliefs and doctrines.

Reversed - Prayers helping, lie low and concentrate, your inner self heals all your ills and troubles, you have your own power within, need a new bed, nurture and nourish yourself now, you have more strength than you think but need to take time for renewal, read

and record your experiences.

5 of Swords

Upright - Arguments, power struggles, envy, jealousy, competition, blame, anger directed towards others or oneself, accusations, punishments, revengeful thinking or actions, strife, shame, defeat, going to war, victory in war, resentment, false pride, hidden enemies, gossip, humiliation.

Reversed - Damaging or hurting others by aggression and force, no conscience or remorse, conversely could mean someone who comes to the aid of another - picks up the pieces and repairs and helps heal wounds or trauma.

6 of Swords

Upright - Moving away from strife or difficulties, moving to a new location, period of positive movement, leaving the past behind, learning from experiences, positive move.

Reversed - Going backwards, unable to move, outer influences causing delay or return to old places or circumstances, feeling of temporary defeat, have to wait until

things shift.

7 of Swords

Upright - Walking away from something before it is finished, sneakiness, cleverness, escapism or avoidance, getting out while the getting is good, stealth, lying or deceiving, cowardice, folly, gossip.

Reversed - Thievery, cheating, abandoning a bad situation, not giving notice, and letting others finish the job.

Upright - Feeling held back, confined or trapped by past or current circumstances, imprisonment, being tied down, being held captive by one's own beliefs or fears or by the opinions of others, need to get out on one's own, possessiveness, soda masochism, outside interferences.

Reversed - Freeing yourself from bondage, walking out or away from a bad or imprisoning situation, saying 'no' to abuse, standing up for oneself, time to take your power back, stop self-pity, decide to be strong, you can do it, stop listening to others who are negative or self-defeating, take blinders off and look ahead. Go forward - take the first steps. Just do it! Get the help you need.

9 of Swords

Upright - Despair, worry, depression, illness, loneliness, mental illness, suicidal tendencies, need for comfort, nightmares, hopelessness, pessimism, could be of one's own distorted thinking, insomnia, all of the above leaving one's life.

Reversed - Headaches, despair increased, eye or back problems, hormone imbalances, poor health, need to stop dwelling on the past or on current anxieties, get help, use protection techniques.

10 of Swords

Upright - Hitting bottom, psychic attacks, ruin, feeling defeated, death, accident, negative cycle that will soon pass, the worst is over.

Reversed - Loss of valuable energy or reserves, others can no longer hurt you, you will soon be renewed, take time to heal, surrender your losses and start over - misfortune could be the beginning of a new and better life.

Page of Swords

Upright - Messages through thought or email, a young person who is astute, mental, observant, intelligent, aware, perceptive, witty, intellectual, analytical, ready to make a move or physically move, good with horses, eloquent speaker, fair-minded.

Reversed - Foolish or rash behavior, decide carefully, be patient and wait, gifted artist or poet, clairvoyant, good teacher.

Knight of Swords

Upright - A youth who is aggressive, forceful, quick to act, compulsive, ready, courageous, sometimes acts without thinking, wants things in a hurry, impatient, progressive, and powerful.

Reversed - Need to take control of a situation, fight for what is right but be fair and just, use caution and then proceed, powerful leadership abilities, use influence wisely.

Queen of Swords

Upright - A woman who is analytical, highly perceptive and intelligent, observant and fair-minded, compassionate, could be a widow or a woman separated or divorced, clear in insight and of a higher mind when positive, decisive, right, knowing, sees through others.

Reversed - Critical or domineering, quick to judge, unfair, opinionated but still highly intelligent, has a soft spot for those in need, expects others to do their best and won't settle for less, strong when challenged, has great endurance.

King of Swords

Upright - A man who is more intellectual and opinionated rather than emotional or sensitive, could be a judge or someone in a position to decide matters, fair and highly reasonable in the positive, can be calm and easy, quiet and observant.

Reversed - Critical and cold in the negative, unfeeling, and judging with limited knowledge and foresight, weak internally, doesn't want the responsibility of leadership or decision-making, silent when he should be speaking up or acting.

SWORD people are usually fair-haired, with any color eyes.

Their astrological signs most often are Gemini, Libra & Aquarius.

Chapter 6:
Meaning of The Cards and Cards Interpretation The Pentacles

Ace of Pentacles

Upright - A new business opportunity or money-making proposition, an increase in self-awareness leading to an increased sense of well-being, start of a new abundant cycle, self-definition, rising above limitations into something more productive, being offered a gift of money.

Reversed - Obstacles to achieving the money you need or desire, being held back by others, self-esteem needs to be boosted, may not be feeling well, misuse of money which is causing lack, repressed energies.

2 of Pentacles

Upright - Financial instability, two or more jobs at once, indecision about financial or work matters, in-between jobs, imbalance or fluctuation in emotions due to financial instability, roller-coaster, being at opposite ends with someone or something, things up in the air.

Reversed - Considering the possibilities, making a decision about the best choice, clarity and strength returning allowing for positive action, may move to a new location, feeling capable once again and in control of one's life and circumstances.

3 of Pentacles

Upright - A new project coming together or finishing the initial stages of a project, apprenticeship, submitting plans for approval, artistry, some expertise gained in some area but there is more to learn, arts and crafts, flea markets or craft fairs, the coming together of a project, work being accepted, take constructive criticism as a positive thing.

Reversed - Delays on the finishing of a project but all will turn out well, take the advice of others who are more experienced, be patient, spiritual guidance will come, keep records and plans on paper, more education may be needed.

Upright - Security gained, status quo, can be a hoarder, limitations in going further, fear to move out of current comfort zone, insecurity on a personal level, inhibited, fear of success, grounded or not grounded, inability to let go, self-defamation, treading on thin ice, rigid behaviors or viewpoints.

Reversed - Throwing caution to the wind, health returning, letting go of a stagnant lifestyle or way of doing things, having the confidence to go further, going back to school or taking a new job or position, may move to a new location, letting go of old fears and restrictions, opening up to new ideas and possibilities.

5 of Pentacles

Upright - Unemployment or job loss, financial hardship or instability, changes in finances, need to reevaluate current lifestyle or conditions, illness possible, seeking guidance, wanting to succeed but having a hard time, needing change, need to bring spirituality back into your life, prepare for cold climate.

Reversed - Spirituality regained, things getting better and moving forward, release of victim consciousness, making a decision for wellness, bring children into your life or do something to help others, to give is to receive.

6 of Pentacles

Upright - Promotions or loans granted, help financially or giving help to someone, generosity, benefactors, gifts, financial balance, gain, rewards, winning something, receiving what is due to you, paying off debts, gratitude is the key to prosperity, balance giving with receiving.

Reversed - Money given but not enough, not feeling deserving, have been put down by others, homeless person or situation, do what you can to find work, any amount of pay will increase your self-esteem, bank loan denied or for a lesser amount than needed, don't lose confidence - you can get back on your feet.

7 of Pentacles

Upright - Material accomplishments, resting period after earned successes or hard work, evaluation before proceeding further, gardening, fruition, vacation, strength and maturity gained, a level of satisfaction and peace achieved.

Reversed - Not satisfied with progress to date, re-evaluating a situation or outcome, a perfectionist who wants to do better, a good crop this year, fertilize soil for fruits and vegetables, working with the earth or environment is a good choice, natural healer - use your
talents and abilities to achieve greater success, gifted with your hands.

8 of Pentacles

The eighth card in the Suit of Pentacles shows a man sitting on a bench, hanging the eight coins on a tree, far away from the distractions he would find at home, i.e. the village in the background. You can see that he is fully immersed in his task and he does not want to make any mistake whatsoever.

Upright Meaning: Dedication, Development of Skills and Focus

When it turns up in an upright position, the Eight of Pentacles can indicate that you are in a learning phase of a new skill or in the next level of a skill you already had. You are fully dedicated to it, and willing to do the same tasks over and over again just so that you can get as close to perfection as you possibly can. You are completely focused on your end goal, and consequently, on the tasks you have at hands. Remember that learning new skills takes time and a few setbacks along the way and keep up the commitment and hard work.

And if you see this card but you are not invested in any new skill or task, it might be time to do just that!

Reversed Meaning: Boredom, Mediocrity and Self-Growth

The Eight of Pentacles reversed might be a sign that you are bored with the repetitive tasks you have to take on in order to achieve greatness. Try to make your tasks harder or to find others on the same level that will teach you the same lessons.

It can also mean that you are not reaching the outcomes you wished for, either because you are not working hard or because the hard work you are putting in is not showing to be effective. Either put in a little bit more effort or change your approach.

Nine of Pentacles

A card full of bright colors, the Nine of Pentacles shows a woman in a long yellow dress and her whole outfit suggests that she is a wealthy woman, as does the big house you can see from afar. She has a falcon calmly sitting on her hand, representative of her intellectual side. Behind her, the coins and grapes grow, representing her achievements, and she is lightly touching them, showing that she has a healthy connection to what she has gained with her successes.

Upright Meaning: Independence, Rewards and Affluence

The Nine of Pentacles upright means that your efforts and all the rewards you have gotten from it have allowed you to be independent, to support yourself without the aid of others, and that can mean financially and/or as an individual, with your spiritual growth. More than anything, this card turns up as a reminder that you should celebrate, do what makes you the happiest and enjoy everything you have worked so hard for to the fullest!

Reversed Meaning: Working Too Hard, Spending Too Much and Self-Care

The Nine of Pentacles reversed can mean that you are working too much and you're harming your wellbeing. This is starting to become a pattern in this suit, but this card can show up as a reminder to take care of yourself. You are the most productive when you are healthier and happier, so don't slack off on those things.

It can also be a sign that you got so comfortable with the abundance that you may have started to spend a little bit too much. Remember that the money you worked so hard for can disappear in the blink of an eye. There is a fine line between spending it on things that you enjoy and splurging. At the very least, make sure to have a savings account that you do not touch unless it is an emergency.

Ten of Pentacles

There is a lot going on in the Ten of Pentacles card. It shows an older man sitting, with his two white dogs in front of him. It also depicts a young couple and their child, who is petting the dog. When we see all these people together, they seem to be three generations of the same family, and the older man is the wise patriarch who has achieved a lot during his younger years and is now able to provide comfort and security to his family.

Upright Meaning: Support, Family and Stable Foundation

The Ten of Pentacles upright is a great family card. Not only do you have each other's backs financially, but if there is something that is not lacking, it is love and affection between everyone.

All the hard work you have been putting into your career has paid off, and you are able to establish a safe foundation for yourself, as well as share it with your loved ones. Seeing them living comfortably makes you extremely happy, especially because you know first-hand what it took to get to where you are now.

As you get to such a stable phase of your life, this card also reminds you to think long term, so that you and your family don't end up losing everything you have now.

Reversed Meaning: Broken Family due to Inheritance-related Conflicts, Financial Loss and Instability

Wealth does not always bring up the best side in people and you might be going through a situation where that is clear. If you are going through disputes with family members because of an inheritance, understand how far you are willing to go for that money and remember that some things are not worth losing, not for any amount of dollars.

This can also suggest that you are going through some difficulties regarding your finances after you had just achieved a good level of comfort, which might be hard to adapt to. However, what you cannot do is keep living the same lifestyle. In order to get back on your feet, reduce your spending and work to go back to the stability.

Page of Pentacles

On the Page of Pentacles card, we can see one single man looking at the coin he is holding, representative of his wealth, comfort and aspiration, he is trying to understand how he can get even more benefits of that kind. In the back, the green scenery suggests affluence and the mountains stand for the setbacks he will come across.

Upright Meaning: New Opportunities, Development of Skills and Manifestation

The Page of Pentacles upright tends to show up when you are looking for new financial opportunities that will allow you to get where you wish to in terms of money and material possessions. It reminds you that in order for you to find them, not only do you have to keep your eyes open, but you have to be determined and willing to put in effort and time into your professional journey.

One way to do that is by learning new skills and/or learning even more surrounding an area you are already familiar with, so that is what this card encourages you to do.

Reversed Meaning: Laziness, Stagnation and Missed Opportunities

The Page of Pentacles reversed comes as a warning sign that you are letting procrastination get in the way of you achieving your objectives, either by not working on your project as much as you should or by not grabbing new opportunities. It invites you to understand why you are being lazy and how you can change that.

It can also mean that you have reached a point of stagnation when it comes to your project, so this might be a good time to either change the approach or distance yourself from it, so that when you come back to it your brain has had time to refresh and hopefully, you will see possible ideas that you did not see before.

Knight of Pentacles

The Knight of Pentacles shows a knight on his black horse, holding a coin while carefully looking at it. This indicates that he is really thinking and planning before he takes any action, which is very different from the other knight cards we have seen before. This knight thinks long term, while others only consider their short-term objectives and possible victories.

Once again, there is a reference to repetitive tasks needed to do in order to succeed, with the fields in the background, but the knight is willing to do them.

Upright Meaning: Planning, Routine and Long-Term Goals

The Knight of Pentacles upright means that you have been applying a more thought-out, rational approach to the way you work, which might delay the moment you take action, but also allows you to make informed decisions. You don't let yourself rush because of your short-term goals; rather, you consider the long-term ones, as you know that those are the ones that will give you a stable foundation in the future. This might mean starting a daily routine that is not the most exciting one, but when you see this card, you can rest assured that you are on the right track.

Reversed Meaning: Irresponsibility, Monotony and Inflexibility

Firstly, the Knight of Pentacles can be a sign that you are not being mature and responsible enough for the work you have to do. Avoid doing things like leaving certain thing for tomorrow when you can do them today and doing things just so they are done, instead of doing them well.

It can also mean that you have gotten bored with the monotony of routine. If so, change it up to make it more exciting, while achieving the same outcomes.

Lastly, it can be a sign that you want everything to be so perfect, that you are lost the ability to be flexible with yourself and with others. This card encourages you to relax and accept the fact that everybody makes mistakes.

Queen of Pentacles

The scene depicted in the Queen of Pentacles happens in nature: The Queen sits on her throne and observes and nurtures the coin she has on her lap (i.e. her wealth). Look closely and you will see a little rabbit at the bottom of the card, representative of her energy and fertility.

Upright Meaning: Success, Nurture and Practicality

The Queen is a very compassionate and nurturing figure, and this card in an upright position represents just that. With the energy, practical thought and calm attitude, you have been treating those around you, you make everyone feel good and loved. And still, you find time to dedicate yourself to your professional life and be continuously successful. You have found the perfect balance.

Reversed Meaning: Unbalance, Inner Conflicts and Self-Care

The Queen of Pentacles in reverse can signify that you are having a hard time balancing your professional life and your personal life, and that is making you feel guilty. Remember that there is time for everything and some adjustments in your time management will make you feel a lot better.

It can also signify that you are taking care of yourself. This is very important in able to achieve success, so even if now you are doing it with bigger gestures - maybe you treated yourself with an expensive massage or you bought a ticket to a country you have always wanted to visit - you should find small ways of treating yourself every single day.

King of Pentacles

• Upright: discipline, self-control, self-mastery, personal power

• Reversed: controlling, abusive, domination

Chapter 7:
Meaning of The Cards and Cards Interpretation Wands

Ace of Wands

It is a sign of expanding consciousness and knowledge. There is a creative process ahead, and new things will be born. This may also state the birth of a new baby as well as a new project or a new idea. In either case, the process is a healthy and productive one. If you put enough effort into it, the progress is inevitable. Reversed, this card symbolizes problems. Because the person is not yet equipped enough to solve them and they might make decisions that are not well thought. Usually, it might mean that the timing is not right for the things that are planned or the person is not mature enough.

Keywords: Activity. Initiative.

Concise direct/positive meaning: Great start! Be as active as you can.

Concise reversed/negative meaning: Premature start. Excessive self-confidence, impulsivity, and adventurism.

Two of Wands

It tells you to listen to your intuition if you are facing a problem. You have the potential of being creative and the potential to be original too. You have all the knowledge for that. The card also means that someone is strong minded and they know how to get ahead of the game. This might sometimes look as over-ambitious, but actually, it is strong willed. It also shows balance and fairness.

Reversed, this card means Indecisiveness which in turn causes to put things on hold for long periods of time. It also symbolizes the lack of originality and not having enough inspiration. Instead of being strong willed, this person can easily be manipulated because they feel weak and they do not have enough self-confidence to make a decision. Usually, they are afraid of doing the wrong thing and being criticized for it.

Keywords: Equal rights. Business partnership.

Concise direct/positive meaning: Successful negotiations. Constructive cooperation.

Concise reversed/negative meaning: Do not compromise. Unsuccessful business partnership. Different interests and points of view.

Three of Wands

This signifies being rewarded for hard work. This is the card of a good outcome when it comes to work. When it comes to a relationship, it indicates someone being picky. But they will be rewarded for it too. For people who are single, it can mean a new romance with someone who will feel like a soulmate, for ongoing relationships, it means that the relationship will move on to a deeper level.

Reversed, this card symbolizes that the person is experiencing delays for the outcome. There are obstacles and blocks in the way. The person might be dealing with something they are not capable of handling because they do not have enough experience. It shows disappointment.

Keywords: News awaiting.

Concise direct/positive meaning: Wait a little more, and you'll get a result.

Concise reversed/negative meaning: Long and pointless waiting.

Four of Wands

This signals a happy event is about to occur. It could be a wedding, engagement. It might also mean the purchase of a new property. It shows an increase in wealth. For people who already have a house, this might mean a second one to use as a vacation home or life in the countryside.

Reversed Four of Wands means the cancellation of plans and change of plans. If there was a plan for a wedding or engagement, there might be problems. The conditions might not yet be ready so you should avoid making important decisions.

Keywords: Celebration, Holiday, crowd.

Concise direct/positive meaning: A deserved success. Rest after a hard day.

Concise reversed/negative meaning: Premature jubilation.

Five of Wands

This signals irritation, opposition, and argument. Especially in teamwork, the need to stand out individually. But it also shows a personality that defends what is right, even if there are people who oppose and disagree. For relationships, it can be an argument. Personality wise it shows problems with authority, self-doubt, and insecurity.

Reversed, this card means not having enough faith for a favorable outcome, thus, not giving enough effort towards it. There is a lack of self-confidence, fear of success and fear of conflict.

Keywords: Chaos.

Concise direct/positive meaning: Don't be afraid of mess and clutter, that is all not for long and won't harm.

Concise reversed/negative meaning: The intrigues, quarrels.

Six of Wands

This symbolizes recognition, feeling good about yourself and feeling achieved. It also symbolizes success and victory. If you have been working on something, this signals a good outcome. You will be pleased with the result. The person for whom this card appears is someone who is popular in his/her circle.

People find this person friendly and approachable. In relationships, it means admiration by their partners. At work, it symbolizes successful projects.

Keywords: Triumph.

Concise direct/positive meaning: Success and confidence.

Concise reversed/negative meaning: Overconfidence, pride. Premature jubilation.

Seven of Wands

This symbolizes a person who is capable of adapting to different situations easily. However, this also indicates a personality that puts up barriers. It is because they prefer to protect themselves and their personal space. This might make other people think that the person is not approachable. In a relationship, it means the person is putting up walls because they are afraid of being hurt.

Reversed, this card means lack of self-defense, inability to take action. When this card is reversed it might also show that something the querent has been working for is falling apart. Or simply not going anywhere.

Keywords: Fight with invisible and obscured enemies.

Concise direct/positive meaning: Skillful protection of one's point of view.

Concise reversed/negative meaning: A person takes a defensive position. He stubbornly defends his point of view though no one tries to persuade him otherwise or attack him.

Eight of Wands

This signals a quick turn of events. This card usually appears when someone is expecting visitors or is planning to go on a trip. It also means that the person is planning to visit someone. For those who are in a relationship, especially a new relationship, this card symbolizes falling in love. If single it might show that the querent will meet someone with whom they will fall in love rather quickly. Career wise it signals a change ahead, in a good way. Reversed, this card means physical exhaustion. Certain things are not going in the right direction at work or in a relationship. Beware of unnecessary arguments.

Keywords: Speed.

Concise direct/positive meaning: Fast and confident actions.

Concise reversed/negative meaning: Slow down. Don't rush headlong.

Nine of Wands

This is about finally finding the courage to do something. Maybe you have wanted to do something but were hesitant to do so. If this is the case, you will feel braver to take the next step. You discover a side of you that is stronger. However, this card also shows you currently do not have enough trust in others. You strongly defend what you believe in, and you are a family-oriented person. You protect your family. In a relationship, this might signal stressful times.

Reversed, this card means you are feeling weak, and you are stubborn. You have thoughts and beliefs, but you do not stand by them, you rather let things be, instead of making an effort to progress.

Keywords: Conclusions the complicated fight. Weariness.

Concise direct/positive meaning: You need to rest and to think.

Concise reversed/negative meaning: Fatigue, apathy. Delay, procrastination in all affairs. Difficulty. Hardships. You should stop waiting and start acting!

Ten of Wands

This symbolizes having more responsibilities than one can handle. It might cause someone to get overwhelmed by it and lose track. You need to remember to focus on the result instead of worrying too much about the little details. If a person is in a relationship, then it means this relationship requires too much effort to keep. If the person is single, then they are more focused on what others will think of them, instead of trying to show their real personality. Reversed, this card symbolizes fear of taking on responsibilities. It could be due to lack of motivation or lack of self-esteem. They do want the experience, but they are at the same time ready to call it quits and walk away.

Keywords: Reload. Powerful tension. The last effort in finalizing of important business.

Concise direct/positive meaning: hard work and diligence will help you overcome any troubles.

Concise reversed/negative meaning: A person took more than one can carry (physical and mental strain). Responsibilities that you cannot manage.

Page of Wands

This means the querent is curious and willing to learn new things and experience different things. There are also new ideas that will come to the surface, but the cards before and after will determine better how the situation will progress. There is an overload of communication. Because this card is about "news" of any kind. It could mean the person is receiving news or they are delivering the news. In a relationship, it means there could be ups and downs as each party is learning to grow.

Usually, people like this attract others who will challenge them both spiritually and intellectually because they love learning. Reversed, this card means lack of enthusiasm and not having enough motivation to learn and experience new things. Instead, the person wants others to pay them attention. If they are in a competitive situation, this is most likely an unhealthy process due to unnecessary drama.

Keywords: Good news. Delight.

Knight of Wands

This denotes a person who loves being the center of attention. But they are the center of attention, whether they try it or not because they have a charming, fun and loving personality. The card also symbolizes high energy, passion, and love. In a love reading, this card shows a relationship that is working well. There are fun and romance and love and passion. The couple might be planning to travel together. Professionally, it means new and exciting job opportunities. But depending on the person's position, it could also mean that this job requires a lot of interaction with people and requires problem-solving skills without being carried away in other people's drama. Reversed, this card means a highly competitive person in a destructive way because they will stop at nothing to get what they want. Revenge, bad temper and bad thoughts should be kept under control.

Keywords: Activity, courage.

Concise direct/positive meaning: Courage and resolution. Active steps.

Queen of Wands

This indicates a warm, likable, passionate personality. Usually, this card appears for people who are interested in metaphysics, supernatural and spiritual things. It also symbolizes an inner journey towards self-discovery. Career wise it can symbolize learning new things to advance. Reversed, this card symbolizes a dominating and intimidating personality. Usually, these people complain about not having real friends. They think everyone around them is superficial and fake, but in fact, they are the ones who push people away with their dramatic personalities.

Keywords: Energy. Generosity.

Concise direct/positive meaning: Success in all affairs. Joy and happiness.

Concise reversed/negative meaning: A self-confident, scandalous, ambitious person. An obtrusive and excessive care. Redundant generosity, extravagance, and the desire to splurge.

King of Wands

• Upright: leadership, valor, honor, successful business ventures

• Reversed: unsatisfied, hasty, expecting too much, ruthlessness, ego

Chapter 8:
Reading for Yourself and For Others

Tarot cards are visual tools to help the subconscious mind perceive messages. Tickets can be used as a mediator between your conscious awareness and the source of information ("God," "Gods," religious leaders, hobbies, angels, ancestors or whatever);

Tarot cards work because they are not magical, and they are well crafted. Magic "you." "You." "You." You're the intangible being who knows more than what you can see, taste, hear, feel, and sense every day. The problem is that you are so aware that your brain can't work, and most of it stops. Peens when you are overwhelmed, and too many people talk at once or when the boss shouts and the radio play while the TV is on (extra loud to compensate for the yells). Your brain tries to shut off a great deal of excess noise to focus on what you decide. If it's too much, the brain tries to shut everything out, so that you can regain the center.

Your overall performance is similar but on a much larger scale. Life calls for survival (sleep and food that do not require experience over time). All of this is a mental disturbance that must make you feel like dreaming, producing "tunnel vision." Its trance-like state is no different from the trance in which all the others are. Therefore, enlightened people "above all," the object of wealth and luxury is the elimination of the psychic psychobabble of everyday life and the enhancement of your consciousness. Ironically, it often leads to people who have a higher level of insanity (untrained in the theory of knowledge), but this time to a deeper level of self-gratification.

You're already psychic. Some don't get a special gift, and some don't. Training is needed, but you can become more conscious of your own destiny and power. Tarot cards are an insight escape when you are able to get rid of all conversation and stress, and they also take you in the right direction to solve problems and answer questions. You can do it with a bunch of players, but it's a lot harder. This is why even centuries after they reject the idea that "rich people are closer to God" rather than the poor (the principle of God's activeness, "Nobility," and aristocracy is mainly rich people who abuse poor people, and poor people who somehow accept it as' right and faithful').

Tarot card images can seem outdated or absurdly obsolete, but they symbolize major human events, motives, and behavior. See the pictures and see with your eyes what is there. The trick is not to memorize a bunch of (non-useful) keywords and words or try to force astrology into cards that do not match.

This maintains the urge of dogs and cats to mate. It's not right! It's not right!

However, what works is throwing away all the superstitions and the myth of reading cards and sitting down and looking at the cards. Get to know them. Get to know them. Get to know them. Get to know them. Hello, everybody, see what the images are telling you. Please reply (It's always best to ask a question, so you know what your cards respond to) and look at the cards.

1) When you are comfortable and open to all texts, it is easier to read tarot cards.

Often said, but not as often clarified. The reason this is so critical is that you are very tempted to test your cards when you hope for results. Sadly, this will only impede your comprehension of the cards, and you will lack their knowledge. I am afraid it does not count as a reading of wishful thinking. If you are worried or worried about a problem, but it is tempting, try to wait for you to remain calmer.

2) The Major Arcana or the Divisions of Minor Arcana have tarot cards.

If you're a novice, you might have a book to hand to help you with your ticket definitions. This is a great idea, but don't lose out on the implications of a set of cards. Major Arcana, for instance, has a stronger message often and can mean that you really have to sit and consider that if one of these cards appears.

The cups usually apply to emotional problems in the Minor Arcana. Know these general rules and concentrate on individual interpretations because they can subtly change your message.

3. You may find it useful to try various spreads for a particular purpose when reading tarot cards, such as love reading.

A tarot spread means that the cards are placed and positioned in accordance with the spread rules selected. The position of the map represents something like the past or present, etc., and yes, it is another way of subtly changing the meaning of the card! The Celtic Cross is a popular tarot spread, but variants can be searched for.

4) Not everybody has a mighty intellectual talent.

Nonetheless, everyone can rely on the latent abilities they all have. This skill will be significantly improved by daily or at least a persistent reading of tarot cards. Each time you ask a specific question, you can notice some pictures or symbols or cards often appear in specific fields. Learn how to accept this new voice— it's yours, and you're different. The first and most reliable response to a question is often psychic intuition, so learn to trust your associations and to be on the right course.

5) Pick your tarot deck carefully.

The Rider-Waite deck is the most popular and reliable and precise, so it is an excellent base for beginners. The Tarot of

Marseilles is another famous one. The main factor is that you have to talk to the symbolism. Have you always been attracted to holidays? Maybe a fairy deck depicting the cards is perfect for you? The same is true if you are still aligned with ancient goddesses. Recall that it is personal to read tarot cards, so move on and understand what you like. Feel free to have several packs to choose a mood-based rack.

6) Tarot can be used to ask questions quickly or to obtain a situation snapshot, but keep your question straight and just select one card. It is perfect, for example, for "how will my day be? For a quick morning read.

7) Did you know you can also use cards in a simple spell while tarot cards are used primarily for divination? Spell candles derive their color power, for example, emitting energy that overcomes specific difficulties? Orange is excellent for creativity.

Chapter 9:
Techniques for Reading Tarot

When you are ready to start practicing spreads, find a few that you are most comfortable with. You only need simple spreads that use a few cards when first starting out. Even the most advanced Tarot readers still find benefit from a three-card spread.

Begin by clearing your cards of energy and shuffling them thoroughly. With any spreads, you'll want to meditate on your question while shuffling. Continue shuffling the cards as you repeat your question until you feel ready to lay them down.

Feel free to cut the deck as many times as you want or have the person you are reading for shuffle and cut them. Find a ritual that gets you in the best head space to analyze and interpret the images you are about to see. You may feel the need to use a "clarifying card." This is when you pull an additional card to provide more context to a spread. You don't want to use this as a crutch, but it can be used when more information is needed.

If you have a friend that's able to help you, try doing this exercise to improve your contrast and comparison abilities. You can use this method of practicing for focusing on the entire deck, the Major Arcana by itself, or the Minor Arcana independently. In any case, you'll start by shuffling the deck. Once shuffled, take the top card and put it in front of you to the right. This is the card for your friend. Then take the next card and place it slightly to the left of the first, as the card that represents what happens to yourself. Perform a mini-reading. Do this again with the next two cards and work your way through the entire deck. This will increase your familiarity with the cards and get you used to look at all the cards equally. We need to remember that these cards are all equal and that we should have any reservations with drawing certain cards. Also, try to come up with different impressions and meanings instead on one rigid definition of each card. Don't spend too much time on any card or pair of cards. You can ask a simple question before each draw, or you can simply perform this exercise to create your own stories for the cards simply.

For even further insight into the relationship of the cards in a spread, pay attention to if they are facing one another or if they are facing away from each other. What type of indications comes up when we take note of the way the figures in the cards are facing? Look through your cards and find figures in each card that are looking towards or away from each other.

Ask yourself the following questions:

● What's the purpose of this interaction?

● Is the subject matter positive or negative?

● Why might they be facing away from each other, or facing each other regarding this scenario or question?

● What are these cards communicating?

● Are they ignoring each other?

Spreads

One Card

As mentioned before, you can simply pull one card a day. Set your intention before you pull the card by asking what energy you need to focus on, or what you might experience in your day. Make a note about what card you drew and what stood out to you about it. At the end of the day, journal any correlations you found.

Three Card Spreads

● Past-Present-Future

Many Three Card spreads relate to the Past, Present, and Future. Place the cards left to right and they will represent the past, present, and future positions. You can find the things that shaped who you are and what's happening in your life now as well as receive an indication of where the energy in your life is leading. Keep in mind that your current actions have the power to change everything.

- Blessings- Challenges- Action

Another Three Card Spread is the Blessings, Challenges, Action spread. If you are seeking clarity regarding the next step, then this spread can be beneficial. Laid the same way as the Past, Present, and Future spread, this shows where you will find help in this situation in the Blessings position. For Challenges, you see what problem you need to solve, or what you're up against. With the Action position, it signifies what you should or should not do to address the challenge.

- Situation- Action- Outcome

In unclear situations, this three-card spread can be particularly helpful. The left card, the Situation, is the thing you've asked about. This may look different than you expected but it will give insight into what's going on. The middle card, the Action card, is a recommendation of the action needed to get to the card on the right, the Outcome card.

Five Card Spread

1. The far-left position, or the bottom, represents the reasons leading to the situation at hand.

2. The left of center position reveals those things in our past that still affect us currently.

3. The center position represents our present situation.

4. This position signifies our future outcomes.

5. The top card is possible outcomes if the course of action is followed.

Celtic Cross Spread

One of the most popular spreads, the Celtic Cross uses 10 cards in a circle/line layout. There are many variations regarding how the cards are laid but they will typically consist of five cards (one in the middle and four cards surrounding it – one on each side of the middle card and one card laid sideways on the center card.). Then a line to the right of those five for cards seven through ten.

1. Center card on the bottom. The first card you lay. It represents the current condition.

2. Center card laid on top of Card #1. Represents your Current Obstacles and Troubles.

3. Above the center card, representing the best outcome possible.

4. To the Right of the center card, representing the cause for the current situation.

5. Below the center card, representing your near past.

6. To the Left of the center card, representing you in the near future.

7. On the Bottom of the Line to the right of the circle. This card represents in general, who you are right now and your relation to the theme of the question.

8. Directly above the preceding card, this position represents your current surroundings as it relates to your question. (environment, family, friends)

9. Directly above the preceding card, representing fears and hopes regarding the situation or your life in general if there is no specific question.

10. The final and top card of the line, this card represents the outcome, or how this phase is turning out.

Horseshoe Spread

A seven-card spread where there is one main card placed in the center and has three cards laid on either side of it forming a staggered version of a horseshoe. This spread is read from left to right.

1. The Past (The first card on the bottom left working towards the Center and down the right side)

2. The Present

3. Hidden Influences

4. You, or the Querent

5. Attitudes of others

6. What you should do

7. The Outcome

There are so many spreads for you to learn, and multiple variations on each one that you should have plenty to practice with. Find which spreads you are comfortable with. You can use certain spreads for certain types of questions, or for deeper understanding in the card's relationships.

You may decide to include reverse cards in your readings, or not. Don't feel pressured to do anything you're not ready to commit to!

Chapter 10:
Choosing Your Cards or Letting the Cards Choose You

At one point in time, there really weren't very many options when it came to choices in tarot decks. There were a few well respected, well-illustrated standard decks available. In fact, if wanted a deck that was really unique, you would be called upon to illustrate it yourself. Times have changed and those days belong in the past. Today, there are so many choices of tarot decks that the process of choosing the right deck for you, especially if it is your first one can feel overwhelming to say the least.

The process of choosing your deck is a highly personal one. Some people find the deck the resonate with right away and that is the only deck they use for years until the images have become so worn and the cards so frayed that the deck is barely recognizable anymore. Others, have a collection of decks, each appealing to them for different reasons and they alternate between all of them. Unfortunately, there is another group that has a collection of tarot decks, but most of them sit around unused because they were purchased, only to realize after working with the cards for a bit that something about the energy didn't feel right. The cards just didn't resonate with the reader. This is not only discouraging, but also costly since some tarot decks can be a little pricey. Therefore, I would like to present you with some advice on choosing your first deck before we even get started talking about the actual cards. I want your experience with tarot to be as positive as possible.

To begin, let's talk about the difference between a tarot deck and an oracle deck. The traditional tarot deck is standardized in many ways. There is a structure that remains in place regardless of the theme or the artwork. A tarot deck contains seventy-eight cards, including twenty-two major arcana cards and fifty-six minor arcana cards. There is an order in which the cards appear, and there is standard symbolism associated with each card regardless of the deck. With tarot cards, the real difference from deck to deck is the artwork and the energy that it puts off. If you love renaissance art, you might not easily relate to a deck that features simple lines and clean modern art. Even though each card has some standard symbolism, the artwork adds new elements to the card. This is why you might get a feeling about, say the World card, in one deck but feel you are getting a very different message from the same card of another deck. You may also find that some decks are easier for you to interpret while others require you actually to study them intuitively. Tarot cards were originally structured to be a game and resemble the suits that you would find in a traditional deck of playing cards today.

Oracle cards are cards that were designed with divination purposes in mind, but their theme and structure is not in any way regulated. There might be twenty cards in an oracle deck, or there might be one-hundred cards. The cards might contain imagery similar to that of the tarot or they might not. Oracle cards are often beautiful and valuable tools for connecting to your inner voice, however you must learn to read each deck independently. There will be no similarity in meanings from one deck to the next. Most oracle decks come with a guide that will help you discover and connect to the symbolism of the cards. A typical tarot guide might be useful for spreads, but it will not offer you much insight into oracle cards in terms of the individual card meanings.

Whichever type of deck feels most comfortable to you is the one that you should use. It is just important that you know the difference because many a novice has wandered in to pick up a tarot only to end up confused and frustrated with trying to use it according to tarot descriptions. The purpose is to discover tarot, so those are the cards that we will focus on, however everything in here, except for the actual card descriptions themselves can be applied to any tarot or oracle deck.

The most important tool you have for choosing your tarot deck is your intuition. Some might say that you should start out with a well-recognized deck, like the Waite deck, which has been studied and used for generations. This isn't bad advice, but personally I feel that you are only going to develop your intuitive powers, which are necessary for reading the tarot, if you feel connected to the imagery of the cards on a deeper level. If a well-known deck does that for you, then great. However, if you feel no connection to that deck, it is best to pass it by and choose one that really resonates with you. Don't be surprised if you end up with a deck that you never would have thought you would choose. Tarot speaks to us on a level that we don't always understand. This is ok, go with what feels right.

If you have a metaphysical store or a bookstore that carries a variety of tarot cards, take a stop in there and look around. Most retail establishments that sell tarot cards have a sample deck of each style set out for you to examine. Take your time and look over each card. Even feeling negatively about one card can affect your overall relationship with the deck. Go through each deck and choose the one that feels most personal. If you are in a position where you are buying your cards online, do a little research and find images of each card before making your decision.

Don't neglect the guide that comes with each deck. In each box of tarot cards is a little booklet that should explain the history of the deck, the philosophy behind it and a brief explanation of card imagery and symbolism.

Take your purpose into consideration. There is a tarot deck out there that fits just about every area of spiritual and metaphysical interest. You might come to tarot because you want more connection with spirit guides or angels. If this is the case, you should choose a deck with imagery that is relevant. The same goes for other interests such as fairies, nature, goddesses, meditation, etc.

Practical matters are important too. The size of the cards and how they feel in your hands are two very important factors to consider when choosing your deck. You don't want the cards to be uncomfortably large in your hands, and likewise you don't want them to be so small that they are awkward to handle. They should be printed on sturdy, high quality card stock. Some decks have a sheen or lamination to them that is meant to serve a serve a protectant, but also make the decks easier to clean.

Decide if you want this feature or if you prefer the more traditional, coarser feel of a matte deck.

Not only does the imagery need to resonate with you, but you also must be able to see and use it. If you have poor eyesight or know that you will be doing readings in a dimly lit environment, choose a deck that is not heavily or ornately illustrated, but has clear pictures and clean lines instead.

Sometimes the deck needs to find you. There is folklore floating around out there that you should never buy your own tarot deck, that instead your cards should be gifted to you. I disagree with this philosophy; however, I do not deny that sometimes the deck will find a way to you, and when it does you should not refuse it.

Finally, if after choosing your deck and working with it for a bit, you aren't feeling a connection to it, please don't get discouraged. Everyone who desires a relationship with tarot can have one, it is just a matter of exploring different decks until you find the ones that opens the door for you.

Chapter 11:
The Most Effective Method to Read Tarot Cards – Your Step-By-Step Guide

1) Align Yourself with the Tarot

Understanding imagery is an incredible begin to figure out how to read tarot cards however the most ideal approach to acclimate yourself with the energies of the cards is to concentrate on them individually.

Inundate yourself in the story by reading the understandings – using a decent source book just as confiding in your own instincts.

Set aside the effort to assimilate the energies of each card, by concentrating on the symbolism, hues, numbers and images.

Keep a Tarot diary and record your impressions of each card.

A few people like to put a card under their pad before resting, then recording their impressions and dreams toward the beginning of the day.

2) Meditate on the Tarot

Seeing as the Tarot is a story, you should utilize your very own account while investigating the cards.

Locate a calm spot where you won't be upset. Beginning with the Major Arcana and working through the Minor Arcana and Court cards, place each card – individually on a table before you.

Reflect on the card and once you've retained the symbolism, close your eyes and consider what that card intends to you.

Give it a chance to happen normally – regardless of whether you feel that your brain is meandering – watch where it proceeds to record your impressions.

Rehearse this with each card and return to this reflection once in a while.

Another reflection is to convey the card with all of you day – particularly if the imagery matches what sort of a day you believe you will have.

You can likewise pick a card that speaks to what you need to occur.

Look out for anything identified with the card and record your encounters once you return home.

3) Use Memorization Tricks

There are 78 cards in the Tarot and incalculable mixes including the large number of various inquiries you may pose, so retaining the entirety of the cards can be an overwhelming one.

Understanding that it will require some investment to get familiar with the numerous aspects of every one of the 78 cards is the initial step.

Split it up into segments to make it progressively serviceable for you, for example, starting with the suits in the minor arcana.

Or then again you may get a kick out of the chance to deal with the Court cards in the first place, then proceed onward to the suits, then to the major arcana.

Anyway, you choose to do it, focus on each segment and once you feel that now is the right time, proceed onward through the deck.

Observe repeating subjects, pictures and mixes that feed significance to one another.

Using watchwords is another valuable strategy for remembering the implications and translations. Think of them in your Tarot diary and submit them to memory.

Imaginative perception is an incredible method to recall that anything, so if you return to reading the Tarot as a story, you'll recollect each card in accordance with the account of the Tarot.

For instance: think about each card as a part – nourishing from the past card and streaming onto the following.

4) Create a Sacred Space

Having a holy space where you can direct your exploration and Tarot readings – deferentially and undisturbed – implies that you will have a superior possibility for adjusting yourself to your cards.

Dispreads a zone where you're more averse to be occupied by other individuals, clamor from the road, TV and so on.

Enrich the region as indicated by how you feel about your hallowed space, the Tarot, otherworldliness and so on.

For some it may be precious stones, plants and silk scarves; for other people, it could be New Age pictures on the divider and incense.

Whatever your decisions, ensure your region is a genuine impression of who you are profoundly.

5) Explore the Tarot Spreads

There are such a significant number of various kinds of Tarot spreads, so it's a smart thought to investigate what works for you.

You will find that it relies upon the kind of reading you will do, regardless of whether it's a short – one inquiry reading or a mind boggling, year spread or Celtic Cross.

If you intend to bargain Tarot cards for other people, get them to rearrange and hand the deck back to you.

Do whatever it takes not to translate the cards as indicated by what you think they need to know and exhort them that you will just be uncovered what the cards state.

Let them know not to tell you what they're asking, which is an incredible method to test the reading and your aptitudes.

In your consecrated space, take your cards and cautiously mix them in the wake of ruminating over the question and explanation behind the reading (except if reading for another person.)

When you feel that you've rearranged well, either fan them out (face down – from left to right) or cut the deck with your correct hand from left to right in case you're just doing a one card spread.

Celtic Cross Spread

Pick (as quick as possible) ten cards from your fanned deck. Beginning from straightforwardly before you, lay the cards as pursues:

Each position spreads an alternate subject or viewpoint in your life, as pursues:

• First Card: Your present position and perspective.

• Second Card: Your test; what crosses you.

• Third Card: Your past, what acquired you to this point time.

• Fourth Card: The not so distant future.

• Fifth Card: Current objectives and desires.

• Sixth Card: The subliminal considerations behind your inquiry; shrouded mysteries.

• Seventh Card: Recommendations and guidance for going ahead.

• Eighth Card: Events or potentially individuals influencing your inquiry; outside your ability to control.

• Ninth Card: Your expectations and fears.

• Tenth Card: Outcome (contemplating your present direction.)

In case you're doing a 6-card spread, you won't have to spread the staying four cards on the correct side of the cross.

In this occasion, the initial 5 cards have indistinguishable implications from above, with the 6th card being your result.

3 Card Spread

As in the past, mix the cards while you think about your inquiry.

You may ask "What is wanting me throughout the following month?" or "Educate me concerning such and such circumstance, individual, occasion and so forth."

Fan the cards out and pick three cards rapidly. Spread them out in a line from left to right.

- First Card: Recent Past.

- Second Card: Where you are presently.

- Third Card: The Outcome.

One Card Reading

In the wake of rearranging the cards and thinking about your inquiry (make it straightforward and immediate, for example, "Will I land the position?" or "Should I confide in my beau/sweetheart?") – slice them from left to right and lift the main card up from the highest point of the uncovered stack.

Translate the appropriate response and mix again and repeat if you need explanation.

12 Month Spread

Rearrange and fan the cards, then pick twelve from left to right (which demonstrates going from the past to the future) and beginning from straightforwardly before you – going clockwise – place the cards face down around.

You'll have to neaten it up once you're finished. Beginning from the main card, turn them over.

The main card speaks to the present month and from the second card onwards, the next months will be spoken to by a card each.

Decipher the reading and record your impressions in your diary.

This is helpful to recollect your reading just as to twofold check when the year is finished.

Here are some more spreads you should play with, from fundamental two card spreads up to five card spreads.

Blend it up to make your own, when you feel great enough to do as such.

6) Interpret the Tarot Reading

Inquiries to pose

Obviously, this all relies upon what's happening in your life at some random time and what you need to think about.

It's imperative to get directly to the point with yourself.

If you as of now have a notion that the relationship you just began will end in tears, a Tarot reading won't offer you interchange responses.

More often than not, us people have a skill for having the option to anticipate what will occur, in light of our chronicles and motivation.

Using the Tarot to approach questions ought to be kept for the occasions when greater issues are close by, instead of for unrealistic reasoning, negligible things like tattle and other unessential subjects.

Keep your inquiries straightforward, for example, "What's desiring me throughout the following year?" or "Is it a smart thought for me to go after this position?"

The most ideal approach to test yourself is to pose extremely fundamental inquiries, so you can guarantee that you don't infuse the cards with a previously modified and wanted result.

Attempt to clear your mind and state unmistakably, "You let me know?"

It's astonishing what can come up when you don't drive the issue or confound the reading to go for whatever you might prefer.

Astonishments and privileged insights can be uncovered when you don't color your inquiries with tangled objectives and ulterior thought processes.

Mixes and Correspondences

As referenced already, it's critical to look at encompassing cards to improve thought about what the message is.

In many cases, readings bode well when every one of the cards are translated – like looking at the woods instead of the trees.

How would they all identify with one another?

Is there a consistent idea?

Now and then you'll see themes, for example, cards being overwhelmingly pentacles or Queens.

If there are a great deal of Major Arcana cards, then the reading means a significant arrangement of occasions coming up.

The mixes are what makes the Tarot a captivating technique for divination, because of the profundity of importance.

Correspondences are the additional components to be remembered for the translations, for example, Astrology and Numerology.

The components of earth, air, fire and water are likewise used.

Visionary affiliations are additionally significant when looking at the Court cards.

Here's a short breakdown of the relating affiliations:

• Pentacles: Taurus, Virgo, and Capricorn

• Swords: Aries, Leo, and Sagittarius

• Wands: Gemini, Libra, and Aquarius

• Cups: Cancer, Scorpio, and Pisces

There are numerous minor departures from the prophetic affiliations and different correspondences, contingent upon the various styles and customs used by Tarot followers – just as the various ways of thinking, where interchange thoughts regarding what component or sign relates to what Tarot card are shifted.

- Pentacles: Element – Earth; matters managing cash, down to earth concerns, security, insurance.

- Wands: Element – Air; matters managing the astuteness, thought, thoughts, insight.

- Swords: Element – Fire; matters managing power, energy, activity, change, sanitization.

- Cups: Element – Water; matters managing feelings, the psyche, imagination, dreams.

Note: a few people say that Wands are the component of fire and that Swords are the component of air.

This is available to translation, however observing as Wands for the most part originate from wood = trees, it's reasonable that the branches waving noticeable all around are ascribed to that component, alongside Swords produced in fire.

CONCLUSION

Now, as you have to go through, now you will come to know how you can read and construct your natal charts and their deeper meanings. This must have explained all the basics of astrology; the history and origin of the astrology make you familiar with the concept of astrological predictions. It has explained all the related tools of astrology that is used by the astrologer for making a prediction. If you are a beginner, you will be able to deal with the astrological aspect.

The main aim of this was to make you aware of the basic concept of astrology and how to use them in the prediction of an individual's birth chart and their personality. It has explained all the possible facts of astrology that you people like the most. I am sure this will definitely help you in learning astrology in a better and easy way.

As you all that the celestial objects present in the universe emit different kind of energy which is directly or indirectly concerned with our daily life activity but mostly, we are not aware of these and neglected by us most of the time. The purpose of this is to tell you about the techniques and tools that are used in astrology to predict the circumstances in your life. The content of this opens your eyes towards the astrological aspects and meaning of each and every celestial object in your life.

The Enneagram sheds light on self-awareness and personal growth. Considering this is a new year, make the decision to look deep inside yourself for the things you like most and the things you would like to change to be a better version of yourself. Learning about your Enneagram personality type is an excellent catalyst to making a positive change in your life. So, what is it going to be for you in 2020? Take a bold step and make a difference in your life. You will thank the Enneagram for aiding in successful personal growth later.

The more that you invest in understanding yourself through crafts like numerology, the easier it is for you to develop yourself along this journey. It is important to understand that tools like numerology are only meant to be used as a guide and not as a strict rule in your life. As you read through your chart and reflect on it, remember that you may find areas where you do not resonate with your chart simply because you are a unique individual. You may find that you can find an even deeper resonance by going back to the double-digit number before the single digit number to help you resonate even deeper. In other numbers, you may completely identify with the primary number and find that it tells you plenty. To summarize, there is so much to be learned about yourself through numerology, but the ultimate learning comes from reflecting on it and seeing how it actually relates to you in your lifetime. This way, you can learn not only about numerology, but about yourself, too.

It is a good idea to write your chart down on paper or in a document so that you can reflect back on it whenever you need to. Many people find that their charts become valuable to them at many points in life, and they reference back to it frequently. As a result, they are able to get great information about how they can move through different phases of their life, what they can expect from the people around them, and how they make better decisions. Regularly reflecting back on your chart can be a valuable opportunity for you to move in alignment with your true soul, which is the biggest benefit of numerology.